Schubert

Piano Trio
in Bb major, Opus 99

Music Minus One 'Cello

MMO
85

TRIO

Trio No. 1 in B♭ major, Op. 99 (D. 898)
for Violin, Cello and Piano

CELLO

Allegro moderato

Franz Peter Schubert

4

Andante un poco mosso

Scherzo
Allegro

Trio

Rondo

Allegro vivace

MMO Compact Disc Catalog

BROADWAY

LES MISERABLES/PHANTOM OF THE OPERA	MMO CD 1016
HITS OF ANDREW LLOYD WEBBER	MMO CD 1054
GUYS AND DOLLS	MMO CD 1067
WEST SIDE STORY 2 CD Set	MMO CD 1100
CABARET 2 CD Set	MMO CD 1110
BROADWAY HEROES AND HEROINES	MMO CD 1121
CAMELOT	MMO CD 1173
BEST OF ANDREW LLOYD WEBBER	MMO CD 1130
THE SOUND OF BROADWAY	MMO CD 1133
BROADWAY MELODIES	MMO CD 1134
BARBRA'S BROADWAY	MMO CD 1144
JEKYLL & HYDE	MMO CD 1151
SHOWBOAT	MMO CD 1160
MY FAIR LADY 2 CD Set	MMO CD 1174
OKLAHOMA	MMO CD 1175
THE SOUND OF MUSIC 2 CD Set	MMO CD 1176
SOUTH PACIFIC	MMO CD 1177
THE KING AND I	MMO CD 1178
FIDDLER ON THE ROOF 2 CD Set	MMO CD 1179
CAROUSEL	MMO CD 1180
PORGY AND BESS	MMO CD 1181
THE MUSIC MAN	MMO CD 1183
ANNIE GET YOUR GUN 2 CD Set	MMO CD 1186
HELLO DOLLY! 2 CD Set	MMO CD 1187
OLIVER 2 CD Set	MMO CD 1189
SUNSET BOULEVARD	MMO CD 1193
GREASE	MMO CD 1196
SMOKEY JOE'S CAFE	MMO CD 1197
MISS SAIGON	MMO CD 1226

CLARINET

MOZART CONCERTO, IN A, K.622	MMO CD 3201
WEBER CONCERTO NO. 1 in Fm. STAMITZ CONC. No. 3 IN Bb	MMO CD 3202
SPOHR CONCERTO NO. 1 in C MINOR OP. 26	MMO CD 3203
WEBER CONCERTO OP. 26, BEETHOVEN TRIO OP. 11	MMO CD 3204
FIRST CHAIR CLARINET SOLOS	MMO CD 3205
THE ART OF THE SOLO CLARINET:	MMO CD 3206
MOZART QUINTET IN A, K.581	MMO CD 3207
BRAHMS SONATAS OP. 120 NO. 1 & 2	MMO CD 3208
WEBER GRAND DUO CONCERTANT WAGNER ADAGIO	MMO CD 3209
SCHUMANN FANTASY OP. 73, 3 ROMANCES OP. 94	MMO CD 3210
EASY CLARINET SOLOS Volume 1 - STUDENT LEVEL	MMO CD 3211
EASY CLARINET SOLOS Volume 2 - STUDENT LEVEL	MMO CD 3212
EASY JAZZ DUETS - STUDENT LEVEL	MMO CD 3213
VISIONS The Clarinet Artistry of Ron Odrich	MMO CD 3214
IN A LEAGUE OF HIS OWN Classic Songs played by Ron Odrich and You	MMO CD 3215
SINATRA SET TO MUSIC Kern, Weill, Gershwin, Howard and You	MMO CD 3216
STRAVINSKY: L'HISTOIRE DU SOLDAT	MMO CD 3217
BEGINNING CONTEST SOLOS - Jerome Bunke, Clinician	MMO CD 3221
BEGINNING CONTEST SOLOS - Harold Wright	MMO CD 3222
INTERMEDIATE CONTEST SOLOS - Stanley Drucker	MMO CD 3223
INTERMEDIATE CONTEST SOLOS - Jerome Bunke, Clinician	MMO CD 3224
ADVANCED CONTEST SOLOS - Stanley Drucker	MMO CD 3225
ADVANCED CONTEST SOLOS - Harold Wright	MMO CD 3226
INTERMEDIATE CONTEST SOLOS - Stanley Drucker	MMO CD 3227
ADVANCED CONTEST SOLOS - Stanley Drucker	MMO CD 3228
ADVANCED CONTEST SOLOS - Harold Wright	MMO CD 3229
BRAHMS Clarinet Quintet in Bm, Op. 115	MMO CD 3230
TEACHER'S PARTNER Basic Clarinet Studies	MMO CD 3231
JEWELS FOR WOODWIND QUINTET	MMO CD 3232
WOODWIND QUINTETS minus CLARINET	MMO CD 3233
FROM DIXIE to SWING	MMO CD 3234
THE VIRTUOSO CLARINETIST Baermann Method, Op. 63 4 CD Set	MMO CD 3240
ART OF THE CLARINET... Baermann Method, Op. 64 4 CD Set	MMO CD 3241
POPULAR CONCERT FAVORITES WITH ORCHESTRA	MMO CD 3242
BAND-AIDS CONCERT BAND FAVORITES WITH ORCHESTRA	MMO CD 3243

PIANO

BEETHOVEN CONCERTO NO. 1 IN C	MMO CD 3001
BEETHOVEN CONCERTO NO. 2 IN Bb	MMO CD 3002
BEETHOVEN CONCERTO NO. 3 IN C MINOR	MMO CD 3003
BEETHOVEN CONCERTO NO. 4 IN G	MMO CD 3004
BEETHOVEN CONCERTO NO. 5 IN Eb (2 CD SET)	MMO CD 3005
GRIEG CONCERTO IN A MINOR OP.16	MMO CD 3006
RACHMANINOFF CONCERTO NO. 2 IN C MINOR	MMO CD 3007
SCHUMANN CONCERTO IN A MINOR	MMO CD 3008
BRAHMS CONCERTO NO. 1 IN D MINOR (2 CD SET)	MMO CD 3009
CHOPIN CONCERTO NO. 1 IN E MINOR OP. 11	MMO CD 3010

MENDELSSOHN CONCERTO NO. 1 IN G MINOR	MMO CD 3011
MOZART CONCERTO NO. 9 IN Eb K.271	MMO CD 3012
MOZART CONCERTO NO. 12 IN A K.414	MMO CD 3013
MOZART CONCERTO NO. 20 IN D MINOR K.466	MMO CD 3014
MOZART CONCERTO NO. 23 IN A K.488	MMO CD 3015
MOZART CONCERTO NO. 24 IN C MINOR K.491	MMO CD 3016
MOZART CONCERTO NO. 26 IN D K.537, CORONATION	MMO CD 3017
MOZART CONCERTO NO. 17 IN G K.453	MMO CD 3018
LISZT CONCERTO NO. 1 IN Eb, WEBER OP. 79	MMO CD 3019
LISZT CONCERTO NO. 2 IN A, HUNGARIAN FANTASIA	MMO CD 3020
J.S. BACH CONCERTO IN F MINOR, J.C. BACH CON. IN Eb	MMO CD 3021
J.S. BACH CONCERTO IN D MINOR	MMO CD 3022
HAYDN CONCERTO IN D	MMO CD 3023
HEART OF THE PIANO CONCERTO	MMO CD 3024
THEMES FROM GREAT PIANO CONCERTI	MMO CD 3025
TSCHAIKOVSKY CONCERTO NO. 1 IN Bb MINOR	MMO CD 3026
ART OF POPULAR PIANO PLAYING, Vol. 1 STUDENT LEVEL	MMO CD 3033
ART OF POPULAR PIANO PLAYING, Vol. 2 STUDENT LEVEL 2 CD Set	MMO CD 3034
'POP' PIANO FOR STARTERS STUDENT LEVEL	MMO CD 3035
DVORAK TRIO IN A MAJOR, OP. 90 "Dumky Trio"	MMO CD 3037
DVORAK QUINTET IN A MAJOR, OP. 81	MMO CD 3038
MENDELSSOHN TRIO IN D MAJOR, OP. 49	MMO CD 3039
MENDELSSOHN TRIO IN C MINOR, OP. 66	MMO CD 3040
BLUES FUSION FOR PIANO	MMO CD 3049
CLAUDE BOLLING SONATA FOR FLUTE AND JAZZ PIANO TRIO	MMO CD 3050
TWENTY DIXIELAND CLASSICS	MMO CD 3051
TWENTY RHYTHM BACKGROUNDS TO STANDARDS	MMO CD 3052
FROM DIXIE to SWING	MMO CD 3053
J.S. BACH BRANDENBURG CONCERTO NO. 5 IN D MAJOR	MMO CD 3054
BACH Cm CONC. - 2 PIANOS / SCHUMANN & VAR., OP. 46 - 2 PIANOS	MMO CD 3055
J.C. BACH Bm CONC./HAYDN C CONCERT./HANDEL CONC. GROSSO-D	MMO CD 3056
J.S. BACH TRIPLE CONCERTO IN A MINOR	MMO CD 3057
FRANCK SYM. VAR. / MENDELSSOHN: CAPRICCO BRILLANT	MMO CD 3058
C.P.E. BACH CONCERTO IN A MINOR	MMO CD 3059
STRETCHIN' OUT-'Comping' with a Jazz Rhythm Section	MMO CD 3060
RAVEL: PIANO TRIO	MMO CD 3061
THE JIM ODRICH EXPERIENCE Pop Piano Played Easy	MMO CD 3062
POPULAR PIANO MADE EASY Arranged by Jim Odrich	MMO CD 3063
SCHUMANN: Piano Trio in D Minor, Opus 63	MMO CD 3064
BEETHOVEN: Trio No. 8 & Trio No. 11, "Kakadu" Variations	MMO CD 3065
SCHUBERT: Piano Trio in Bb Major, Opus 99 (2 CD Set)	MMO CD 3066
SCHUBERT: Piano Trio in Eb Major, Opus 100 (2 CD Set)	MMO CD 3067
DVORAK QUINTET in A Major, Opus 81 Minus Piano	MMO CD 3068

PIANO - FOUR HANDS

RACHMANINOFF Six Scenes .... 4-5th year	MMO CD 3027
ARENSKY 6 Pieces, STRAVINSKY 3 Easy Dances ... 2-3rd year	MMO CD 3028
FAURE: The Dolly Suite	MMO CD 3029
DEBUSSY: Four Pieces	MMO CD 3030
SCHUMANN Pictures from the East .... 4-5th year	MMO CD 3031
BEETHOVEN Three Marches .... 4-5th year	MMO CD 3032
MOZART COMPLETE MUSIC FOR PIANO FOUR HANDS 2 CD Set	MMO CD 3036
MAYKAPAR First Steps, OP. 29 .... 1-2nd year	MMO CD 3041
TSCHAIKOVSKY: 50 Russian Folk Songs	MMO CD 3042
BIZET: 12 Children's Games	MMO CD 3043
GRETCHANINOFF: ON THE GREEN MEADOW	MMO CD 3044
POZZOLI: SMILES OF CHILDHOOD	MMO CD 3045
DIABELLI: PLEASURES OF YOUTH	MMO CD 3046
SCHUBERT: FANTASIA & GRAND SONATA	MMO CD 3047

VIOLIN

BRUCH CONCERTO NO. 1 IN G MINOR OP.26	MMO CD 3100
MENDELSSOHN CONCERTO IN E MINOR	MMO CD 3101
TSCHAIKOVSKY CONCERTO IN D OP. 35	MMO CD 3102
BACH DOUBLE CONCERTO IN D MINOR	MMO CD 3103
BACH CONCERTO IN A MINOR, CONCERTO IN E	MMO CD 3104
BACH BRANDENBURG CONCERTI NOS. 4 & 5	MMO CD 3105
BACH BRANDENBURG CONCERTO NO. 2, TRIPLE CONCERTO	MMO CD 3106
BACH CONCERTO IN DM, (FROM CONCERTO FOR HARPSICHORD)	MMO CD 3107
BRAHMS CONCERTO IN D OP. 77	MMO CD 3108
CHAUSSON POEME, SCHUBERT RONDO	MMO CD 3109
LALO SYMPHONIE ESPAGNOLE	MMO CD 3110
MOZART CONCERTO IN D K.218, VIVALDI CON. AM OP.3 NO.6	MMO CD 3111
MOZART CONCERTO IN A K.219	MMO CD 3112
WIENIAWSKI CON. IN D. SARASATE ZIGEUNERWEISEN	MMO CD 3113
VIOTTI CONCERTO NO. 22 IN A MINOR	MMO CD 3114
BEETHOVEN 2 ROMANCES, SONATA NO. 5 IN F "SPRING SONATA"	MMO CD 3115
SAINT-SAENS INTRODUCTION & RONDO,	
MOZART SERENADE K. 204, ADAGIO K.261	MMO CD 3116
BEETHOVEN CONCERTO IN D OP. 61 (2 CD SET)	MMO CD 3117
THE CONCERTMASTER - Orchestral Excerpts	MMO CD 3118
AIR ON A G STRING Favorite Encores with Orchestra Easy Medium	MMO CD 3119
CONCERT PIECES FOR THE SERIOUS VIOLINIST Easy Medium	MMO CD 3120

MMO Music Group • 50 Executive Boulevard, Elmsford, New York 10523, 1-(800) 669-7464
Website: www. minusone.com • E-mail: mmomus@aol.com

4/20/98 MMO

1

MMO Compact Disc Catalog

____ 18TH CENTURY VIOLIN PIECES	MMO CD 3121
____ ORCHESTRAL FAVORITES - Volume 1 - Easy Level	MMO CD 3122
____ ORCHESTRAL FAVORITES - Volume 2 - Medium Level	MMO CD 3123
____ ORCHESTRAL FAVORITES - Volume 3 - Med to Difficult Level	MMO CD 3124
____ THE THREE B'S BACH/BEETHOVEN/BRAHMS	MMO CD 3125
____ Double Concerto Op. 3 No. 8	MMO CD 3126
____ VIVALDI-THE FOUR SEASONS (2 CD Set)	MMO CD 3127
____ VIVALDI Concerto in Eb, Op. 8, No. 5. ALBINONI Concerto in A	MMO CD 3128
____ VIVALDI Concerto in E, Op. 3, No. 12. Concerto in C Op. 8, No.6 "Il Piacere"	MMO CD 3129
____ SCHUBERT Three Sonatinas	MMO CD 3130
____ HAYDN String Quartet Op. 76 No. 1	MMO CD 3131
____ HAYDN String Quartet Op. 76 No. 2	MMO CD 3132
____ HAYDN String Quartet Op. 76 No. 3 "Emperor"	MMO CD 3133
____ HAYDN String Quartet Op. 76 No. 4 "Sunrise"	MMO CD 3134
____ HAYDN String Quartet Op. 76 No. 5	MMO CD 3135
____ HAYDN String Quartet Op. 76 No. 6	MMO CD 3136
____ BEAUTIFUL MUSIC FOR TWO VIOLINS 1st position, vol. 1	MMO CD 3137★
____ BEAUTIFUL MUSIC FOR TWO VIOLINS 2nd position, vol. 2	MMO CD 3138★
____ BEAUTIFUL MUSIC FOR TWO VIOLINS 3rd position, vol. 3	MMO CD 3139★
____ BEAUTIFUL MUSIC FOR TWO VIOLINS 1st, 2nd, 3rd position, vol. 4	MMO CD 3140★

★Lovely folk tunes and selections from the classics, chosen for their melodic beauty and technical value. They have been skillfully transcribed and edited by Samuel Applebaum, one of America's foremost teachers.

____ HEART OF THE VIOLIN CONCERTO	MMO CD 3141
____ TEACHER'S PARTNER Basic Violin Studies 1st year	MMO CD 3142
____ DVORAK STRING TRIO "Terzetto", OP. 74 2 violins/viola	MMO CD 3143
____ SIBELIUS: Concerto in D minor, Op. 47	MMO CD 3144
____ THEMES FROM THE MAJOR VIOLIN CONCERTI	MMO CD 3145
____ STRAVINSKY: L'HISTOIRE DU SOLDAT	MMO CD 3146
____ RAVEL: PIANO TRIO MINUS VIOLIN	MMO CD 3147
____ GREAT VIOLIN MOMENTS	MMO CD 3148
____ RAGTIME STRING QUARTETS The Zinn String Quartet	MMO CD 3151
____ SCHUMANN: Piano Trio in D minor, Opus 63	MMO CD 3152
____ BEETHOVEN: Trio No. 8 & Trio No. 11, "Kakadu" Variations	MMO CD 3153
____ SCHUBERT: Piano Trio in Bb Major, Opus 99 Minus Violin (2 CD Set)	MMO CD 3154
____ SCHUBERT: Piano Trio in Eb Major, Opus 100 Minus Violin (2 CD Set)	MMO CD 3155
____ BEETHOVEN: STRING QUARTET	MMO CD 3156
____ DVORAK QUINTET in A major, Opus 81 Minus Violin	MMO CD 3157
____ BEETHOVEN: STRING QUARTET No. 1 in F major, Opus 18	MMO CD 3158

GUITAR

____ BOCCHERINI Quintet No. 4 in D "Fandango"	MMO CD 3601
____ GIULIANI Quintet in A Op. 65	MMO CD 3602
____ CLASSICAL GUITAR DUETS	MMO CD 3603
____ RENAISSANCE & BAROQUE GUITAR DUETS	MMO CD 3604
____ CLASSICAL & ROMANTIC GUITAR DUETS	MMO CD 3605
____ GUITAR AND FLUTE DUETS Volume 1	MMO CD 3606
____ GUITAR AND FLUTE DUETS Volume 2	MMO CD 3607
____ BLUEGRASS GUITAR	MMO CD 3608
____ GEORGE BARNES GUITAR METHOD Lessons from a Master	MMO CD 3609
____ HOW TO PLAY FOLK GUITAR 2 CD Set	MMO CD 3610
____ FAVORITE FOLKS SONGS FOR GUITAR	MMO CD 3611
____ FOR GUITARS ONLY! Jimmy Raney Small Band Arrangements	MMO CD 3612
____ TEN DUETS FOR TWO GUITARS Geo. Barnes/Carl Kress	MMO CD 3613
____ PLAY THE BLUES GUITAR A Dick Weissman Method	MMO CD 3614
____ ORCHESTRAL GEMS FOR CLASSICAL GUITAR	MMO CD 3615

FLUTE

____ MOZART Concerto No. 2 in D, QUANTZ Concerto in G	MMO CD 3300
____ MOZART Concerto in G K.313	MMO CD 3301
____ BACH Suite No. 2 in B Minor	MMO CD 3302
____ BOCCHERINI Concerto in D, VIVALDI Concerto in G Minor "La Notte", MOZART Andante for Strings	MMO CD 3303
____ HAYDN Divertimento, VIVALDI Concerto in D Op. 10 No. 3 "Bullfinch", FREDERICK THE GREAT Concerto in C	MMO CD 3304
____ VIVALDI Conc. in F; TELEMANN Conc. in D; LECLAIR Conc. in C	MMO CD 3305
____ BACH Brandenburg No. 2 in F, HAYDN Concerto in D	MMO CD 3306
____ BACH Triple Concerto, VIVALDI Concerto in D Minor	MMO CD 3307
____ MOZART Quartet in F, STAMITZ Quartet in F	MMO CD 3308
____ HAYDN 4 London Trios for 2 Flutes & Cello	MMO CD 3309
____ BACH Brandenburg Concerti Nos. 4 & 5	MMO CD 3310
____ MOZART 3 Flute Quartets in D, A and C	MMO CD 3311
____ TELEMANN Suite in A Minor, GLUCK Scene from 'Orpheus', PERGOLESI Concerto in G (2 CD Set)	MMO CD 3312
____ FLUTE SONG: Easy Familiar Classics	MMO CD 3313
____ VIVALDI Concerti in D, G, and F	MMO CD 3314
____ VIVALDI Concerti in A Minor, G, and D	MMO CD 3315
____ EASY FLUTE SOLOS Beginning Students Volume 1	MMO CD 3316
____ EASY FLUTE SOLOS Beginning Students Volume 2	MMO CD 3317
____ EASY JAZZ DUETS Student Level	MMO CD 3318
____ FLUTE & GUITAR DUETS Volume 1	MMO CD 3319
____ FLUTE & GUITAR DUETS Volume 2	MMO CD 3320
____ BEGINNING CONTEST SOLOS Murray Panitz	MMO CD 3321
____ BEGINNING CONTEST SOLOS Donald Peck	MMO CD 3322

____ INTERMEDIATE CONTEST SOLOS Julius Baker	MMO CD 3323
____ INTERMEDIATE CONTEST SOLOS Donald Peck	MMO CD 3324
____ ADVANCED CONTEST SOLOS Murray Panitz	MMO CD 3325
____ ADVANCED CONTEST SOLOS Julius Baker	MMO CD 3326
____ INTERMEDIATE CONTEST SOLOS Donald Peck	MMO CD 3327
____ ADVANCED CONTEST SOLOS Murray Panitz	MMO CD 3328
____ ADVANCED CONTEST SOLOS Julius Baker	MMO CD 3329
____ BEGINNING CONTEST SOLOS Doriot Anthony Dwyer	MMO CD 3330
____ INTERMEDIATE CONTEST SOLOS Doriot Anthony Dwyer	MMO CD 3331
____ ADVANCED CONTEST SOLOS Doriot Anthony Dwyer	MMO CD 3332
____ FIRST CHAIR SOLOS with Orchestral Accompaniment	MMO CD 3333
____ TEACHER'S PARTNER Basic Flute Studies 1st year	MMO CD 3334
____ THE JOY OF WOODWIND MUSIC	MMO CD 3335
____ JEWELS FOR WOODWIND QUINTET	MMO CD 3336
____ TELEMANN TRIO IN F/Bb MAJOR/HANDEL SON.#3 IN C MAJOR	MMO CD 3340
____ MARCELLO/TELEMANN/HANDEL SONATAS IN F MAJOR	MMO CD 3341
____ BOLLING: SUITE FOR FLUTE/JAZZ PIANO TRIO	MMO CD 3342
____ HANDEL / TELEMANN SIX SONATAS 2 CD Set	MMO CD 3343
____ BACH SONATA NO. 1 in B MINOR/KUHLAU E MINOR DUET (2 CD set)	MMO CD 3344
____ KUHLAU TRIO in Eb MAJOR/BACH Eb AND A MAJOR SONATA (2 CD set)	MMO CD 3345
____ PEPUSCH SONATA IN C / TELEMANN SONATA IN Cm	MMO CD 3346
____ QUANTZ TRIO SONATA IN Cm / BACH GIGUE / ABEL SON. 2 IN F	MMO CD 3347
____ TELEMANN CONCERTO NO. 1 IN D / CORRETTE SONATA IN E MINOR	MMO CD 3348
____ TELEMANN TRIO IN F / Bb MAJOR / HANDEL SON. #3 IN C MAJOR	MMO CD 3349
____ MARCELLO / TELEMANN / HANDEL SONATAS IN F MAJOR	MMO CD 3350
____ CONCERT BAND FAVORITES WITH ORCHESTRA	MMO CD 3351
____ BAND-AIDS CONCERT BAND FAVORITES WITH ORCHESTRA	MMO CD 3352

RECORDER

____ PLAYING THE RECORDER Folk Songs of Many Nations	MMO CD 3337
____ LET'S PLAY THE RECORDER Beginning Children's Method	MMO CD 3338
____ YOU CAN PLAY THE RECORDER Beginning Adult Method	MMO CD 3339

FRENCH HORN

____ MOZART Concerti No. 2 & No. 3 in Eb. K. 417 & 447	MMO CD 3501
____ BAROQUE BRASS AND BEYOND	MMO CD 3502
____ MUSIC FOR BRASS ENSEMBLE	MMO CD 3503
____ MOZART Sonatas for Two Horns	MMO CD 3504
____ BEGINNING CONTEST SOLOS Mason Jones	MMO CD 3511
____ BEGINNING CONTEST SOLOS Myron Bloom	MMO CD 3512
____ INTERMEDIATE CONTEST SOLOS Dale Clevenger	MMO CD 3513
____ INTERMEDIATE CONTEST SOLOS Mason Jones	MMO CD 3514
____ ADVANCED CONTEST SOLOS Myron Bloom	MMO CD 3515
____ ADVANCED CONTEST SOLOS Dale Clevenger	MMO CD 3516
____ INTERMEDIATE CONTEST SOLOS Mason Jones	MMO CD 3517
____ ADVANCED CONTEST SOLOS Myron Bloom	MMO CD 3518
____ INTERMEDIATE CONTEST SOLOS Dale Clevenger	MMO CD 3519
____ FRENCH HORN WOODWIND MUSIC	MMO CD 3520
____ MASTERPIECES FOR WOODWIND QUINTET	MMO CD 3521
____ FRENCH HORN UP FRONT BRASS QUINTETS	MMO CD 3522
____ HORN OF PLENTY BRASS QUINTETS	MMO CD 3523
____ BAND-AIDS CONCERT BAND FAVORITES WITH ORCHESTRA	MMO CD 3524

TRUMPET

____ THREE CONCERTI: HAYDN, TELEMANN, FASCH	MMO CD 3801
____ TRUMPET SOLOS Student Level Volume 1	MMO CD 3802
____ TRUMPET SOLOS Student Level Volume 2	MMO CD 3803
____ EASY JAZZ DUETS Student Level	MMO CD 3804
____ MUSIC FOR BRASS ENSEMBLE Brass Quintets	MMO CD 3805
____ FIRST CHAIR TRUMPET SOLOS with Orchestral Accompaniment	MMO CD 3806
____ THE ART OF THE SOLO TRUMPET with Orchestral Accompaniment	MMO CD 3807
____ BAROQUE BRASS AND BEYOND Brass Quintets	MMO CD 3808
____ THE COMPLETE ARBAN DUETS all of the classic studies	MMO CD 3809
____ SOUSA MARCHES PLUS BEETHOVEN, BERLIOZ, STRAUSS	MMO CD 3810
____ BEGINNING CONTEST SOLOS Gerard Schwarz	MMO CD 3811
____ BEGINNING CONTEST SOLOS Armando Ghitalla	MMO CD 3812
____ INTERMEDIATE CONTEST SOLOS Robert Nagel, Soloist	MMO CD 3813
____ INTERMEDIATE CONTEST SOLOS Gerard Schwarz	MMO CD 3814
____ ADVANCED CONTEST SOLOS Robert Nagel, Soloist	MMO CD 3815
____ CONTEST SOLOS Armando Ghitalla	MMO CD 3816
____ INTERMEDIATE CONTEST SOLOS Gerard Schwarz	MMO CD 3817
____ ADVANCED CONTEST SOLOS Robert Nagel, Soloist	MMO CD 3818
____ ADVANCED CONTEST SOLOS Armando Ghilalla	MMO CD 3819
____ BEGINNING CONTEST SOLOS Raymond Crisara	MMO CD 3820
____ BEGINNING CONTEST SOLOS Raymond Crisara	MMO CD 3821
____ INTERMEDIATE CONTEST SOLOS Raymond Crisara	MMO CD 3822
____ TEACHER'S PARTNER Basic Trumpet Studies 1st year	MMO CD 3823
____ TWENTY DIXIELAND CLASSICS	MMO CD 3824
____ TWENTY RHYTHM BACKGROUNDS TO STANDARDS	MMO CD 3825
____ FROM DIXIE TO SWING	MMO CD 3826
____ TRUMPET PIECES BRASS QUINTETS	MMO CD 3827

MMO Music Group • 50 Executive Boulevard, Elmsford, New York 10523, 1-(800) 669-7464
Website: www. minusone.com • E-mail: mmomus@aol.com

2

4/20/98 MMO

MMO Compact Disc Catalog

_____ MODERN BRASS QUINTETS ....MMO CD 3828
_____ WHEN JAZZ WAS YOUNG The Bob Wilber All Stars ....MMO CD 3829
_____ CONCERT BAND FAVORITES WITH ORCHESTRA ....MMO CD 3831
_____ BAND-AIDS CONCERT BAND FAVORITES WITH ORCHESTRA ....MMO CD 3832
_____ BRASS TRAX The Trumpet Artistry Of David O'Neill ....MMO CD 3833
_____ TRUMPET TRIUMPHANT The Further Adventures Of David O'Neill ......MMO CD 3834
_____ STRAVINSKY: L'HISTOIRE DU SOLDAT ....MMO CD 3835
_____ 12 CLASSIC JAZZ STANDARDS Bb/Eb/Bass Clef........................MMO CD 7010
_____ 12 MORE CLASSIC JAZZ STANDARDS Bb/Eb/Bass Clef...............MMO CD 7011

TROMBONE

_____ TROMBONE SOLOS Student Level Volume 1 ....MMO CD 3901
_____ TROMBONE SOLOS Student Level Volume 2 ....MMO CD 3902
_____ EASY JAZZ DUETS Student Level ....MMO CD 3903
_____ BAROQUE BRASS & BEYOND Brass Quintets ....MMO CD 3904
_____ MUSIC FOR BRASS ENSEMBLE Brass Quintets ....MMO CD 3905
_____ UNSUNG HERO George Roberts ....MMO CD 3906
_____ BIG BAND BALLADS George Roberts ....MMO CD 3907
_____ STRAVINSKY: L'HISTOIRE DU SOLDAT ....MMO CD 3908
_____ BEGINNING CONTEST SOLOS Per Brevig ....MMO CD 3911
_____ BEGINNING CONTEST SOLOS Jay Friedman ....MMO CD 3912
_____ INTERMEDIATE CONTEST SOLOS Keith Brown, Professor, Indiana U. ....MMO CD 3913
_____ INTERMEDIATE CONTEST SOLOS Jay Friedman ....MMO CD 3914
_____ ADVANCED CONTEST SOLOS Keith Brown, Professor, Indiana University ..MMO CD 3915
_____ ADVANCED CONTEST SOLOS Per Brevig ....MMO CD 3916
_____ ADVANCED CONTEST SOLOS Keith Brown, Professor, Indiana University ..MMO CD 3917
_____ ADVANCED CONTEST SOLOS Jay Friedman ....MMO CD 3918
_____ ADVANCED CONTEST SOLOS Per Brevig ....MMO CD 3919
_____ TEACHER'S PARTNER Basic Trombone Studies 1st year ....MMO CD 3920
_____ TWENTY DIXIELAND CLASSICS ....MMO CD 3924
_____ TWENTY RHYTHM BACKGROUNDS TO STANDARDS ....MMO CD 3925
_____ FROM DIXIE TO SWING ....MMO CD 3926
_____ STICKS & BONES BRASS QUINTETS ....MMO CD 3927
_____ FOR TROMBONES ONLY MORE BRASS QUINTETS ....MMO CD 3928
_____ POPULAR CONCERT FAVORITES The Stuttgart Festival Band ....MMO CD 3929
_____ BAND-AIDS CONCERT BAND FAVORITES WITH ORCHESTRA ....MMO CD 3930
_____ 12 CLASSIC JAZZ STANDARDS Bb/Eb/Bass Clef........................MMO CD 7010
_____ 12 MORE CLASSIC JAZZ STANDARDS Bb/Eb/Bass Clef...............MMO CD 7011

TENOR SAXOPHONE

_____ TENOR SAXOPHONE SOLOS Student Edition Volume 1 ....MMO CD 4201
_____ TENOR SAXOPHONE SOLOS Student Edition Volume 2 ....MMO CD 4202
_____ EASY JAZZ DUETS FOR TENOR SAXOPHONE............................MMO CD 4203
_____ FOR SAXES ONLY Arranged by Bob Wilber ....MMO CD 4204
_____ BLUES FUSION FOR SAXOPHONE ....MMO CD 4205
_____ JOBIM BRAZILIAN BOSSA NOVAS with STRINGS ....MMO CD 4206
_____ TWENTY DIXIE CLASSICS ....MMO CD 4207
_____ TWENTY RHYTHM BACKGROUNDS TO STANDARDS ....MMO CD 4208
_____ PLAY LEAD IN A SAX SECTION ....MMO CD 4209
_____ DAYS OF WINE & ROSES Sax Section Minus You ....MMO CD 4210
_____ FRENCH & AMERICAN SAXOPHONE QUARTETS ....MMO CD 4211
_____ CONCERT BAND FAVORITES WITH ORCHESTRA ....MMO CD 4212
_____ BAND AIDS CONCERT BAND FAVORITES ....MMO CD 4213
_____ OPEN SESSION WITH THE GREG BURROWS QUINTET ....MMO CD 4214
_____ 12 CLASSIC JAZZ STANDARDS Bb/Eb/Bass Clef........................MMO CD 7010
_____ 12 MORE CLASSIC JAZZ STANDARDS Bb/Eb/Bass Clef...............MMO CD 7011

CELLO

_____ DVORAK Concerto in B Minor Op. 104 (2 CD Set) ....MMO CD 3701
_____ C.P.E. BACH Concerto in A Minor ....MMO CD 3702
_____ BOCCHERINI Concerto in Bb, BRUCH Kol Nidrei ....MMO CD 3703
_____ TEN PIECES FOR CELLO ....MMO CD 3704
_____ SCHUMANN Concerto in Am & Other Selections ....MMO CD 3705
_____ CLAUDE BOLLING Suite For Cello & Jazz Piano Trio ....MMO CD 3706
_____ RAVEL: PIANO TRIO MINUS CELLO ....MMO CD 3707
_____ RAGTIME STRING QUARTETS ....MMO CD 3708
_____ SCHUMANN: Piano Trio in D Minor, Opus 63 ....MMO CD 3709
_____ BEETHOVEN: Piano Trio For Cello ....MMO CD 3710
_____ SCHUBERT: Piano Trio in Bb Major, Opus 99 Minus Cello (2 CD Set) ......MMO CD 3711
_____ SCHUBERT: Piano Trio in Eb Major, Opus 100 Minus Cello (2 CD Set) ......MMO CD 3712
_____ BEETHOVEN: STRING QUARTET ....MMO CD 3713
_____ DVORAK QUINTET in A Major, Opus 81 Minus Cello ....MMO CD 3714

OBOE

_____ ALBINONI Concerti in Bb, Op. 7 No. 3, No. 6, D. Op. 9 No. 2 in Dm ....MMO CD 3400
_____ TELEMANN Conc. in Fm; HANDEL Conc. in Bb; VIVALDI Conc.in Dm .....MMO CD 3401
_____ MOZART Quartet in F K.370, STAMITZ Quartet in F Op. 8 No. 3 ....MMO CD 3402
_____ BACH Brandenburg Concerto No. 2, Telemann Con. in Am ....MMO CD 3403

_____ CLASSIC SOLOS FOR OBOE Delia Montenegro, Soloist ....MMO CD 3404
_____ MASTERPIECES FOR WOODWIND QUINTET ....MMO CD 3405
_____ THE JOY OF WOODWIND QUINTETS ....MMO CD 3406
_____ PEPUSCH SONATAS IN C/TELEMANN SONATA IN Cm ....MMO CD 3407
_____ QUANTZ TRIO SONATA IN Cm/BACH GIGUE/ABEL SONATAS IN F ....MMO CD 3408

ALTO SAXOPHONE

_____ ALTO SAXOPHONE SOLOS Student Edition Volume 1 ....MMO CD 4101
_____ ALTO SAXOPHONE SOLOS Student Edition Volume 2. ....MMO CD 4102
_____ EASY JAZZ DUETS FOR ALTO SAXOPHONE ....MMO CD 4103
_____ FOR SAXES ONLY Arranged Bob Wilber ....MMO CD 4104
_____ JOBIM BRAZILIAN BOSSA NOVAS with STRINGS ....MMO CD 4106
_____ UNSUNG HEROES FOR ALTO SAXOPHONE..............................MMO CD 4107
_____ BEGINNING CONTEST SOLOS Paul Brodie, Canadian Soloist .....MMO CD 4111
_____ BEGINNING CONTEST SOLOS Vincent Abato ....MMO CD 4112
_____ INTERMEDIATE CONTEST SOLOS Paul Brodie, Canadian Soloist ....MMO CD 4113
_____ INTERMEDIATE CONTEST SOLOS Vincent Abato ....MMO CD 4114
_____ ADVANCED CONTEST SOLOS Paul Brodie. Canadian Soloist ....MMO CD 4115
_____ ADVANCED CONTEST SOLOS Vincent Abato ....MMO CD 4116
_____ ADVANCED CONTEST SOLOS Paul Brodie, Canadian Soloist ....MMO CD 4117
_____ Basic Studies for Alto Sax TEACHER'S PARTNER 1st year level ....MMO CD 4119
_____ ADVANCED CONTEST SOLOS Vincent Abato ....MMO CD 4118
_____ PLAY LEAD IN A SAX SECTION ....MMO CD 4120
_____ DAYS OF WINE & ROSES/SENSUAL SAX ....MMO CD 4121
_____ TWENTY DIXIELAND CLASSICS ....MMO CD 4124
_____ TWENTY RHYTHM BACKGROUNDS TO STANDARDS ....MMO CD 4125
_____ CONCERT BAND FAVORITES WITH ORCHESTRA ....MMO CD 4126
_____ BAND AIDS CONCERT BAND FAVORITES ....MMO CD 4127
_____ MUSIC FOR SAXOPHONE QUARTET ....MMO CD 4128
_____ 12 CLASSIC JAZZ STANDARDS Bb/Eb/Bass Clef........................MMO CD 7010
_____ 12 MORE CLASSIC JAZZ STANDARDS Bb/Eb/Bass Clef...............MMO CD 7011

SOPRANO SAXOPHONE

_____ FRENCH & AMERICAN SAXOPHONE QUARTETS ....MMO CD 4801
_____ 12 CLASSIC JAZZ STANDARDS Bb/Eb/Bass Clef........................MMO CD 7010
_____ 12 MORE CLASSIC JAZZ STANDARDS Bb/Eb/Bass Clef...............MMO CD 7011

BARITONE SAXOPHONE

_____ MUSIC FOR SAXOPHONE QUARTET ....MMO CD 4901
_____ 12 CLASSIC JAZZ STANDARDS Bb/Eb/Bass Clef........................MMO CD 7010
_____ 12 MORE CLASSIC JAZZ STANDARDS Bb/Eb/Bass Clef...............MMO CD 7011

VOCAL

_____ SCHUBERT GERMAN LIEDER - High Voice, Volume 1 ....MMO CD 4001
_____ SCHUBERT GERMAN LIEDER - Low Voice, Volume 1 ....MMO CD 4002
_____ SCHUBERT GERMAN LIEDER - High Voice, Volume 2 ....MMO CD 4003
_____ SCHUBERT GERMAN LIEDER - Low Voice, Volume 2 ....MMO CD 4004
_____ BRAHMS GERMAN LIEDER - High Voice ....MMO CD 4005
_____ BRAHMS GERMAN LIEDER - Low Voice ....MMO CD 4006
_____ EVERYBODY'S FAVORITE SONGS - High Voice, Volume 1 ....MMO CD 4007
_____ EVERYBODY'S FAVORITE SONGS - Low Voice, Volume 1 ....MMO CD 4008
_____ EVERYBODY'S FAVORITE SONGS - High Voice, Volume 2 ....MMO CD 4009
_____ EVERYBODY'S FAVORITE SONGS - Low Voice, Volume 2 ....MMO CD 4010
_____ 17th/18th CENT. ITALIAN SONGS - High Voice, Volume 1 ....MMO CD 4011
_____ 17th/18th CENT. ITALIAN SONGS - Low Voice, Volume 1 ....MMO CD 4012
_____ 17th/18th CENT. ITALIAN SONGS - High Voice, Volume 2 ....MMO CD 4013
_____ 17th/18th CENT. ITALIAN SONGS - Low Voice, Volume 2 ....MMO CD 4014
_____ FAMOUS SOPRANO ARIAS ....MMO CD 4015
_____ FAMOUS MEZZO-SOPRANO ARIAS ....MMO CD 4016
_____ FAMOUS TENOR ARIAS ....MMO CD 4017
_____ FAMOUS BARITONE ARIAS...MMO CD 4018
_____ FAMOUS BASS ARIAS ....MMO CD 4019
_____ WOLF GERMAN LIEDER FOR HIGH VOICE ....MMO CD 4020
_____ WOLF GERMAN LIEDER FOR LOW VOICE ....MMO CD 4021
_____ STRAUSS GERMAN LIEDER FOR HIGH VOICE ....MMO CD 4022
_____ STRAUSS GERMAN LIEDER FOR LOW VOICE ....MMO CD 4023
_____ SCHUMANN GERMAN LIEDER FOR HIGH VOICE ....MMO CD 4024
_____ SCHUMANN GERMAN LIEDER FOR LOW VOICE ....MMO CD 4025
_____ MOZART ARIAS FOR SOPRANO ....MMO CD 4026
_____ VERDI ARIAS FOR SOPRANO ....MMO CD 4027
_____ ITALIAN ARIAS FOR SOPRANO ....MMO CD 4028
_____ FRENCH ARIAS FOR SOPRANO ....MMO CD 4029
_____ ORATORIO ARIAS FOR SOPRANO ....MMO CD 4030
_____ ORATORIO ARIAS FOR ALTO ....MMO CD 4031
_____ ORATORIO ARIAS FOR TENOR ....MMO CD 4032
_____ ORATORIO ARIAS FOR BASS ....MMO CD 4033
_____ BEGINNING SOPRANO SOLOS Kate Hurney ....MMO CD 4041
_____ INTERMEDIATE SOPRANO SOLOS Kate Hurney ....MMO CD 4042

MMO Music Group • 50 Executive Boulevard, Elmsford, New York 10523, 1-(800) 669-7464
Website: www. minusone.com • E-mail: mmomus@aol.com

4/20/98 MMO

3

MMO Compact Disc Catalog

MMO Music Group • 50 Executive Boulevard, Elmsford, New York 10523, 1-(800) 669-7464
Website: www. minusone.com • E-mail: mmomus@aol.com

4/20/98 MMO

MUSIC MINUS ONE COMPLETE CATALOGUE

ALL LISTENERS
- MMO TP 7 Understanding Jazz

ALTO SAXOPHONE
- MMO 1045 Top Of The Chart
- MMO 4006 For Saxes Only
- MMO 4017 Lee Konitz Sax Duets
- MMO 4022 20 Dixieland Classics
- MMO 4027 20 Rhythm Backgrounds
- MMO 4031 Swingin' The Classics
- MMO 4036 Two Much! 16 Jazz Duets
- MMO 4037 Sweet Sixteen Jazz Duets
- MMO 4043 How About You?
- MMO 4046 Makin' Whoopee!
- MMO 4051 'Little Jazz Duets'   minus Alto Sax
- MMO 4056 Duet Yourself
- MMO 4056 Two by Four   Jazz Duets in the Round
- MMO 6005 Music For Brass Ensemble
- MMO 7022 Easy Solos For Alto Sax
- MMO 7027 Easy Alto Sax Solos #2
- MMO 7032 More Easy Alto Sax Solos
- MMO 7037 Easy Classics For Alto Sax
- MMO 7044 Have Band — Will Travel
- MMO 7051 Band Aids
- MMO 7057 Popular Concert Favorites
- MMO 7061 Solos With Concert Band
- MMO 7065 Concert Band Classics
- MMO 7069 Sousa Marches minus Alto Sax
- MMO 7080 On Parade (Sousa & others)
- MMO 7086 Concert Band Encores
- MMO TP 4 Basic Saxophone Studies for the student
- See also Vol. 1-1024 Rhythm Backgrounds
- See also MMO 601-606 Rhythm Backgrounds

BASSOON
- MMO 104 Beethoven/Mozart Piano-With Quintets
- MMO 144 Solos For The Bassoon Player
- MMO 148 Beeth., Haydn, Colomer, Mozart, Lefebvre Quintets

BASS VIOLIN
- MMO 15 Schubert Trout Quintet
- MMO 27 Solos For The Double Bass Player
- MMO 7040 The Melodious Bass 60 titles
- See also Vol. 1-1024 Rhythm Backgrounds
- See also MMO 601-606 Rhythm Backgrounds
- See also Vol. 1046/4023/402?

BROADWAY MUSICALS
- MMO 1025 Camelot   Orchestra Backgrounds
- MMO 1030 My Fair Lady   Orchestra Backgrounds
- MMO 1031 Oklahoma   Orchestra Backgrounds
- MMO 1034 Sound Of Music   Orchestra Backgrounds
- MMO 1035 South Pacific   Orchestra Backgrounds
- MMO 1036 The King And I   Orchestra Backgrounds
- MMO 1037 Fiddler On The Roof

'CELLO
- MMO 24 Schumann Piano Quintet, Op. 44
- MMO 25 Solos For The 'Cello Player
- MMO 53 Mendelssohn Piano Trios, Op. 49/66
- MMO 93 Beethoven 6 Piano Trios 3 lps
- MMO 93-1 Beethoven Piano Trios, Op. 1 No. 1/2
- MMO 93-2 Beethoven Piano Trios, Op. 1 No. 3/Op. 11
- MMO 93-3 Beethoven Piano Trios, Op. 70 Nos. 1/2
- MMO 304 Schumann Conc. in a/Saint-Saens/ Faure/Mendelssohn
- MMO 5019 C. P. E. Bach Concerto in A minor
- MMO 5020 Boccherini Conc./Bruch Kol Nidrei

CLARINET
- MMO 61 Brahms Clarinet Quintet Bb clar.
- MMO 62 Clarinet Cameos 9 selections with orch.
- MMO 71 Mozart Clarinet Quintet A/Bb clar.
- MMO 103 Beethoven/Mozart Piano-Wind Quintets
- MMO 113 The Clarinetist—23 selections—piano acc.
- MMO 114 Weber Concertino/Beethoven Trio, Op. 11
- MMO 115 Mozart Concerto in A
- MMO 116 Solos For the Clarinet Player—piano acc.
- MMO 133 First Chair Clarinet Solos—with Orch.
- MMO 134 Art of the Solo Clarinet—with Orch.
- MMO 147 Beeth., Haydn, Colomer, Mozart, Lefebvre Quintets
- MMO 1044 Top Of The Charts
- MMO 4006 For Saxes Only! (or Clarinet)
- MMO 4021 20 Dixieland Classics
- MMO 4026 20 Rhythm Backgrounds
- MMO 4030 Swingin' The Classics
- MMO 4034 Join Me 16 Jazz Duets
- MMO 4035 Two's Company 16 Jazz Duets
- MMO 4042 Solo Spotlight 12 rhythm backgrounds
- MMO 4045 Fools Rush In 12 rhythm backgrounds
- MMO 4050 'Little Jazz Duets'   minus Clarinet
- MMO 4055 Two by Four   Jazz Duets in the Round
- MMO 7021 Easy Solos For The Clarinet
- MMO 7026 Easy Clarinet Solos #2
- MMO 7031 More Easy Clarinet Solos
- MMO 7036 Easy Classics For Clarinet
- MMO 7042 Have Band—Will Travel
- MMO 7049 Band Aids
- MMO 7056 Popular Concert Favorites
- MMO 7060 Solos With Concert Band
- MMO 7064 Concert Band Classics
- MMO 7068 Sousa Marches minus Clarinet
- MMO 7079 On Parade (Sousa Marches plus others)*
- MMO 7085 Concert Band Encores
- MMO TP 2 Basic Clarinet Studies for the student
- See also Vol. 1-1024 Rhythm Backgrounds
- See also MMO 601-606 Rhythm Backgrounds

COMBO ORGAN
- MMO 1043 Top Of The Charts
- MMO 4024 20 Dixieland Classics
- MMO 4029 20 Rhythm Backgrounds

DRUMS
- MMO 125 Fun With Drumsticks
- MMO 170 The Drum Method (basics to Beatles)
- MMO 175 Fun With Brushes
- MMO 4001 Modern Jazz Drumming
- MMO 4002 For Drummers Only!
- MMO 4003 8 Men In Search of a Drummer
- MMO 4004 Drummer Delights
- MMO 4005 Blue Drums (trio sans drummer)
- MMO 4013 Jazz Drumming Live!

EAR TRAINING
- Rutgers University Music Dictation Series 10 lps

GUITAR
- MMO 50 How To Play The Folk Guitar 2 lps
- MMO 60 Let Me Teach You Play The Guitar 2 lps
- MMO 130 How To Play The Electric Guitar
- MMO 140 How To Play The Blues Guitar
- MMO 150 How To Play The Ukulele
- MMO 160 Favorite Folk Songs minus Guitar
- MMO 1041 Top Of The Charts
- MMO 4009 For Guitarists Only!
- MMO 4011 Ten Duets For Two Guitars
- MMO 4012 Classic Guitar Duets
- MMO 4018 'Gene Leis Guitar Duets
- MMO 4049 More Classic Guitar Duets with Rodrigo Riera

FLUTE
- MMO 32 Flute Song 9 selections with orch.
- MMO 106 Mozart 3 Quartets in D/A/C
- MMO 107 Handel Son. G/F/e Telemann Son. D/G/A
- MMO 108 Bach Son. in b Kuhlau Duets in e/D
- MMO 109 Kuhlau Trio Eb Bach Son. Eb/A
- MMO 110 Telemann A min. Suite/Gluck "Orpheus" scene Pergolesi Concerto in G
- MMO 111 Solos For The Flute Player—piano acc.
- MMO 112 Mozart Flute Concerto in G
- MMO 118 Vivaldi Son. in a/Telemann Son. in Bb Boismortier Son. in E minor
- MMO 119 Mozart Flute Quintet (from Clar. quintet)
- MMO 126 Mozart Conc. in D/Quantz Conc. in G
- MMO 127 Bach Suite No. 2 in B minor
- MMO 128 Telemann Six Sonatas for 2 Flutes in Canon
- MMO 129 Beethoven 1st Sym./Leonore Overture Haydn Clock Sym. #101
- MMO 131 Beethoven 2nd Sym./7th Sym.
- MMO 132 C. P. E. Bach Concerto in A minor
- MMO 135 First Chair Flute Solos
- MMO 138 Bach Brandenburg Concerti #4 and #5
- MMO 141 Haydn/Vivaldi/Fred. The Great Flute Concerti
- MMO 142 Telemann/Boccherini Flute Concerti
- MMO 145 Beeth., Haydn, Colomer, Mozart, Lefebvre Quintets
- MMO 4040 17 Jazz Duets For Two Flutes
- MMO 4053 'Little Jazz Duets'   minus Flute
- MMO 4058 'More Flute Duets'   minus Flute
- MMO 7020 Easy Solos For The Flute
- MMO 7025 Easy Flute Solos #2
- MMO 7030 More Easy Flute Solos
- MMO 7035 Easy Classics For Flute
- MMO 7041 Have Band—Will Travel
- MMO 7048 Band—Aids
- MMO 7055 Popular Concert Favorites
- MMO 7059 Solos With Concert Band
- MMO 7063 Concert Band Classics
- MMO 7083 Concert Band Encores
- MMO TP 1 Basic Flute Studies for the student

FRENCH HORN
- MMO 105 Beethoven/Mozart Piano-With Quintets
- MMO 149 Beeth., Haydn, Colomer, Mozart, Lefebvre Quintets
- MMO 6002 Music For Brass Ensemble
- MMO 6009 Mozart: 12 Sonatas for 2 Horns
- MMO 6010 Solos For The French Horn Player
- MMO 7053 Band—Aids
- MMO 7087 Concert Band Encores

HARMONICA
- MMO 1014 Play The Harmonica (Includes Instrument)
- MMO 1047 Blues Harmonica Method (Incl. Chromatic Harm.)

MELLOPHONE
- MMO 6005 Music For Brass Ensemble

OBOE
- MMO 117 Solos For The Oboe Player—15 selections
- MMO 143 Mozart/Stamitz Oboe Quartets
- MMO 146 Beeth., Haydn, Colomer, Mozart, Lefebvre Quintets
- MMO 301 Handel/Telemann/Vivaldi Concerti
- MMO 7084 Concert Band Encores
- MMO 7091 Concert Band Favorites For Oboe*
- MMO 7092 Oboe Solos With Concert Band*
- MMO 7093 Concert Band Classics For Oboe*
- MMO 7094 Airs For Oboe

PIANO
- MMO 11 Schubert "Trout" Quintet, Op. 114
- MMO 21 Schumann Piano Quintet, Op. 44
- MMO 31 Brahms Piano Quartet in g
- MMO 51 Mendelssohn Piano Trios, Op. 49/66
- MMO 81 Schubert Piano Trio, Opus 99
- MMO 82 Schubert Piano Trio, Opus 100
- MMO 101 Beethoven/Mozart Piano-Wind Quintets
- MMO 132 C. P. E. Bach Conc. in a/Haydn Divertimento in Bb
- MMO 300 Tschaikovsky Concerto No. 1 in Bb min., Op. 23
- MMO 303 Liszt Conc. #1 in Eb/Weber Konzerstuck, Op. 79
- MMO 309 Mozart Concerto #20 in d, K. 466
- MMO 309 Mozart Concerto #26 in A, K. 537
- MMO 311 Haydn Concerto in D major
- MMO 312 Grieg Concerto in A minor, Op. 16
- MMO 315 Beethoven Conc. #1 in c, Op. 15
- MMO 315 Beethoven Conc. #3 in C, Op. 37
- MMO 316 Beethoven Conc. #2 in Bb, Op. 19
- MMO 317 Bach Concerto in D minor
- MMO 323 Mozart Concerto in A, K. 488
- MMO 324 Mendelssohn Conc. #1 in G minor
- MMO 325 Beethoven Conc. in D, Op. 61
- MMO 326 Schumann Concerto in A minor
- MMO 327 Mendelssohn Cappriccio/Franck Sym. Var.
- MMO 328 Mozart Concerto in Eb minor, K. 271
- MMO 331 Bach Brandenburg #5/ C. P. E. Bach Conc. in a
- MMO 332 Bach/Schumann Concerti for 2 Pianos & Orch.
- MMO 333 Rachmaninoff Concerto No. 2 in C minor
- MMO 334 Beethoven Concerto #5 in Eb, Op. 73
- MMO 335 Mozart Concerto #24 in c, K. 491
- MMO 336 Beethoven Concerto #4 in G, Opus 58
- MMO 338 Mozart Piano Conc. #3 in G
- MMO 341 Heart of the Piano Concerto
- MMO 342 Great Piano Concerto Themes
- MMO 401 Tschaikovsky 50 Russian Folk Songs—4 hands
- MMO 402 Mozart Complete 4 hand Piano Music 2 lps
- MMO 403 Schubert: Fantasy in f/Bb Son. (4 Hands)
- MMO 1042 Top Of The Charts
- MMO 4007 For Pianists Only! (Popular Songs)
- MMO 4008 They Laughed When I Sat Down To Play (Pop Songs)
- MMO 4014 Jan August Play Along 2 lps
- MMO 4015 Jan August Piano Techniques
- MMO 4016 The Art of Popular Piano Playing
- MMO 4024 20 Dixieland Classics
- MMO 4029 20 Rhythm Backgrounds
- MMO 5023 Haydn Piano Trios (3) in F#, F and G
- MMO 5024 Mozart Piano Quartets #1 in g/#2 in Eb

RECORDER
- MMO 201 Folk Songs of Many Nations minus Alto
- MMO 202 Folk Songs of Many Nations minus Soprano
- MMO 202R How To Play The Recorder (includes Soprano Rec.)
- MMO 203 Telemann Four Duets minus Alto
- MMO 204 Mattheson Eight Trios minus Alto

SINGERS & MUSICIANS
Includes Lyrics/Chords and Music For C/Bb/Eb and Bass Clef Instr.
- MMO 1 Rhythm Section Backgrounds
- MMO 2 Rhythm Section Backgrounds
- MMO 3 Rhythm Section Backgrounds
- MMO 4 Rhythm Section—Gershwin Songs
- MMO 5 Rhythm Section—C. Porter Songs
- MMO 6 Orch. Backgrounds—Rodgers & Hart
- MMO 7 Orchestral Backgrounds
- MMO 8 Rhythm Section—Rodgers & Hart
- MMO 9 Rhythm Section Backgrounds
- MMO 10 Rhythm Backgrounds in 2 Keys (high and low)
- MMO 1001 Orchestral Backgrounds To Standards
- MMO 1002 Rhythm Backgrounds in 2 Keys (high and low)
- MMO 1003 Rhythm Backgrounds in 2 Keys (high and low)
- MMO 1004 Sing With A Band
- MMO 1005 Rhythm Section Backgrounds
- MMO 1006 Rhythm Section Backgrounds
- MMO 1007 Rhythm Section Backgrounds
- MMO 1008 Evolution of the Blues
- MMO 1009 Dixie Anyone?
- MMO 1010 The Dixie Do-It-Yourself
- MMO 1011 The Blues Minus You
- MMO 1012 Moonglow & Stardust plus other R. S. B.
- MMO 1013 Sing or Play With A Band
- MMO 1015 Music of Duke Ellington R. S. B.
- MMO 1016 Music of Jimmy McHugh R. S. B.
- MMO 1017 Music of Nacio Brown R. S. B.
- MMO 1018 Ruby & Laura plus other R. S. B.
- MMO 1019 Music of Harry Warren R. S. B.
- MMO 1020 Hymns of Devotion—Organ Backgrounds
- MMO 1021 Sing or Play Along R. S. B.
- MMO 1022 Sing or Swing With A Band
- MMO 1023 The Gershwin/Porter Songbook-Band Backgrounds
- MMO 1024 Latin American Rhythms
- MMO 601 Rhythm Backgrounds Low Priced Folios
- MMO 602 Rhythm Backgrounds Low Priced Folios
- MMO 603 Rhythm Backgrounds Low Priced Folios
- MMO 604 Rhythm Backgrounds Low Priced Folios
- MMO 605 Rhythm Backgrounds Low Priced Folios
- MMO 606 Rhythm Backgrounds Low Priced Folios
- MMO 651 You Sing The Million Sellers Vol. 1
- MMO 852 You Sing The Million Sellers Vol. 2

TENOR SAXOPHONE
- MMO 1044 Top Of The Charts
- MMO 4006 For Saxes Only!
- MMO 4021 20 Dixieland Classics
- MMO 4026 20 Rhythm Backgrounds
- MMO 4030 Swingin' The Classics
- MMO 4038 Tenor Sax Jazz Duets
- MMO 4039 Tenor Duets 16 Jazz Duets
- MMO 4042 Solo Spotlight 12 rhythm backgrounds
- MMO 4045 Fools Rush In + 11 other standards
- MMO 4052 'Little Jazz Duets'   minus Tenor Sax
- MMO 4057 Two by Four   Jazz Duets in the Round
- MMO 7045 Have Band—Will Travel
- MMO 7052 Band—Aids
- MMO 7088 Concert Band Encores

TROMBONE
- MMO 137 First Chair Trombone Solos
- MMO 1046 Top Of The Charts
- MMO 4023 20 Dixieland Classics
- MMO 4028 20 Rhythm Backgrounds
- MMO 4044 12 Rhythm Backgrounds To Standards
- MMO 4047 '. . . they laughed when I sat down to play'
- MMO 6003 Music For Brass Ensemble
- MMO 6007 Solos For The Trombone—16 selections
- MMO 7024 Easy Solos For The Trombone
- MMO 7029 Easy Trombone Solos #2
- MMO 7034 More Easy Trombone Solos
- MMO 7039 Easy Classics For Trombone
- MMO 7047 Have Band—Will Travel
- MMO 7054 Band Aids
- MMO 7090 Concert Band Encores*
- MMO TP 5 Basic Trombone Studies for the student

TRUMPET
- MMO 136 First Chair Trumpet Solos
- MMO 1044 Top Of The Charts
- MMO 4010 For Horns Only!
- MMO 4021 20 Dixieland Classics
- MMO 4026 20 Rhythm Backgrounds
- MMO 4030 Swingin' The Classics
- MMO 4038 Tenor Sax Jazz Duets
- MMO 4041 Trumpet Duets In Jazz
- MMO 4042 Solo Spotlight 12 rhythm backgrounds
- MMO 4045 Fools Rush In
- MMO 4054 'Little Jazz Duets'   minus Trumpet
- MMO 4059 Two by Four Jazz Duets in the Round
- MMO 6001 Music For Brass Ensemble
- MMO 6006 Solos For The Trumpet Player
- MMO 6008 Haydn/Telemann/Fasch Concerti
- MMO 7023 Easy Solos For Trumpet
- MMO 7028 Easy Trumpet Solos #2
- MMO 7033 More Easy Trumpet Solos
- MMO 7038 Easy Classics For Trumpet
- MMO 7043 Have Band—Will Travel
- MMO 7050 Band—Aids
- MMO 7058 Popular Concert Favorites
- MMO 7062 Solos With Concert Band
- MMO 7066 Concert Band Classics
- MMO 7070 Sousa Marches minus Trumpet
- MMO 7081 On Parade (Sousa & others)
- MMO 7087 Concert Band Encores
- MMO TP 3 Basic Trumpet Studies for the student

TUBA
- MMO 6004 Music For Brass Ensemble

VIOLA
- MMO 11 Schubert "Trout" Quintet, Op. 114
- MMO 23 Schumann Piano Quintet, Op. 44
- MMO 26 Solos For The Viola Player

VIOLIN
- MMO 12 Schubert "Trout" Quintet, Op. 114
- MMO 22 Schumann Piano Quintet, Op. 44
- MMO 52 Mendelssohn Piano Trios, Op. 49/66
- MMO 92 Beethoven 6 Piano Trios 3 lps
- MMO 92-1 Beethoven Piano Trios, Op. 1 Nos. 1/2
- MMO 92-2 Beethoven Piano Trios, Op. 1 No. 3/Op. 11
- MMO 92-3 Beethoven Piano Trios, Op. 70 Nos. 1/2
- MMO 106 Mozart 3 Quartets, D/A/C
- MMO 107 Handel 3 Sonatas Telemann 3 Sonatas
- MMO 139 Mozart Concerti #4/#5
- MMO 302 Sibelius Concerto in D minor
- MMO 305 Mendelssohn Concerto in E minor
- MMO 306 Handel Conc. in b/Sonatas #3 and #6
- MMO 307 Bach "Double" Concerto in D minor
- MMO 310 Bach Concerti in A minor and E major
- MMO 313 Mozart Conc. 4 in D/Vivaldi Conc. in a, Op. 3 #6
- MMO 318 Mozart 2 Romances/"Spring" Son. #5 in F
- MMO 319 Bach Concerto in D minor
- MMO 321 Beethoven Concerto in D, Op. 61
- MMO 322 Mozart Concerto in A, K. 219
- MMO 329 Saint-Saens Intro. & Rondo Cappriccioso Mozart Serenade K. 204/Adagio K. 261
- MMO 330 Bruch Concerto in G minor
- MMO 338 Mozart Concerto #3 in G, K. 216
- MMO 339 Viotti Concerto #22 in A
- MMO 340 Brahms Concerto in D, Opus 77
- MMO 501/2/3 Haydn 6 String Quartets, Op. 76 3 lps
- MMO 501 Haydn String Quartets, Op. 76 Nos. 1/2
- MMO 502 Haydn String Quartets, Op. 76 Nos. 3/4
- MMO 503 Haydn String Quartets, Op. 76 Nos. 5/6
- MMO 5001 Mozart 3 Divertimenti for Strings, K. 136/7/8
- MMO 5002 Mischa Elman Favorite Encores
- MMO 5003 Mischa Elman Concert Favorites
- MMO 5004 Mozart String Quartet, No. 16 in Eb, K. 428
- MMO 5005 Jascha Heifetz Favorite Encores
- MMO 5006 Fritz Kreisler Favorite Encores
- MMO 5007 Solos For The Violin Player
- MMO 5008 Mozart Two Duos For Violin
- MMO 5009 Mozart Adagio and Rondo; Sonata #1 in A
- MMO 5010 Mozart Sonata #4 in G; Sonata #6 in G
- MMO 5011 Schubert Three Sonatas in D/a/g
- MMO 5012 Mozart Son. #10 and #15 in Bb major
- MMO 5013 Tartini Son. in g/Veracini Son. in e
- MMO 5014 Vitali Chaconne/Nardini Sonata in D
- MMO 5015 Mozart Son. #8 in C/Son. #11 in G
- MMO 5016 Mozart Trio #5 in G/Two Sonatinas
- MMO 5017 Haydn Trios #29/30/31 in F/D/G
- MMO 5018 Beethoven Str. Quartets #1 in F/#4 in c
- MMO 5021 Air On A G String (favorite encores with Orch.)
- MMO 5022 Concert Pieces for the Serious Violinist
- MMO 5025 Handel Six Sonatas for Violin and Piano
- MMO 5026 18th Century Violin Music
- MMO 5027 Violin Favorites with Orchestra Easy
- MMO 5028 Violin Favorites with Orchestra Vol. 2 Medium
- MMO 5029 Violin Favorites with Orchestra Vol. 3 Med.-Diff.
- MMO 5030 Beethoven: Sonatas #1 in D and #8 in G
- MMO TP 6 Basic Violin Studies for the student

VOICE   Lieder/Opera/Oratorio

MMO 7001	Schubert Songs	vol. 1	minus high voice
MMO 7002	Schubert Songs	vol. 1	minus low voice
MMO 7003	Schubert Songs	vol. 2	minus high voice
MMO 7004	Schubert Songs	vol. 2	minus low voice
MMO 7005	Brahms Songs		minus high voice
MMO 7006	Brahms Songs		minus low voice
MMO 7007	Favorite Songs	vol. 1	minus high voice
MMO 7008	Favorite Songs	vol. 1	minus low voice
MMO 7009	Favorite Songs	vol. 2	minus high voice
MMO 7010	Favorite Songs	vol. 2	minus low voice
MMO 7011	Italian Art Songs	vol. 1	minus high voice
MMO 7012	Italian Art Songs	vol. 1	minus low voice
MMO 7013	Italian Art Songs	vol. 2	minus high voice
MMO 7014	Italian Art Songs	vol. 2	minus low voice
MMO 7015	Soprano Opera Arias		minus soprano
MMO 7016	Mezzo Opera Arias		minus mezzo
MMO 7017	Tenor Opera Arias		minus tenor
MMO 7018	Baritone Opera Arias		minus baritone
MMO 7019	Bass Opera Arias		minus bass
MMO 7071	Hugo Wolf Songs		minus high voice
MMO 7072	Hugo Wolf Songs		minus low voice
MMO 7073	Richard Strauss Songs		minus high voice
MMO 7074	Richard Strauss Songs		minus low voice
MMO 7075	Oratorio Arias		minus soprano
MMO 7076	Oratorio Arias		minus alto
MMO 7077	Oratorio Arias		minus tenor
MMO 7078	Oratorio Arias		minus bass
MMO 7101	Schumann Songs		minus high voice
MMO 7102	Schumann Songs		minus low voice
MMO 7103	Mozart Arias		minus soprano
MMO 7104	Verdi Arias		minus soprano
MMO 7105	Italian Arias		minus soprano
MMO 7106	French Arias		minus soprano

PRICE SCHEDULE

All MMO Editions are $5.95 each except
- MMO 601 thru 606 .... $1.98 ea.
- MMO 125, 130, 140, 150, 160, 170, 175 .... $3.98 ea.
- MMO 202R/402 .... $11.90 ea.
- MMO 1047 .... $14.95 ea.
- MMO 501-2-3, 92, 93 (3 lp set) .... $17.85 ea.
- Rutgers Ear Training Course (10 lp set) .... $50.00 ea.

Unless noted, all Concerti are performed with full orchestra. MMO Editions come complete with printed music for the missing part.

MMO
MUSIC MINUS ONE
43 WEST 61 ST.
NEW YORK, N.Y.
10023

Copyright 1968 Ramapo Music/BMI
Printed In U. S. A.